TERRIER TROUBLE!

And More True Stories of Animals Behaving Badly!

Candice Ransom

NATIONAL GEOGRAPHIC

WASHINGTON, D.C.

Since 1888, the National Geographic Society has funded more than 12,000 research, exploration, and preservation projects around the world. The Society receives funds from National Geographic Partners, LLC, funded in part by your purchase. A portion of the proceeds from this book supports this vital work. To learn more, visit natgeo.com/info.

NATIONAL GEOGRAPHIC and Yellow Border Design are trademarks of the National Geographic Society, used under license.

For more information, visit nationalgeographic.com, call 1-800-647-5463, or write to the following address:

National Geographic Partners
1145 17th Street N.W.
Washington, D.C. 20036-4688 U.S.A.

Visit us online at
nationalgeographic.com/books

For librarians and teachers:
ngchildrensbooks.org

More for kids from National Geographic:
kids.nationalgeographic.com

For information about special discounts for bulk purchases, please contact National Geographic Books Special Sales:
specialsales@natgeo.com

For rights or permissions inquiries, please contact National Geographic Books Subsidiary Rights: bookrights@natgeo.com

Designed by Ruth Ann Thompson

National Geographic supports K–12 educators with ELA Common Core Resources. Visit natgeoed.org/commoncore for more information.

Library of Congress Cataloging-in-Publication Data

Names: Ransom, Candice F., 1952- author. | National Geographic Society (U.S.)
Title: Terrier trouble! / by Candice Ransom.
Description: Washington, D.C. : National Geographic Kids, [2017] | Series: National geographic kids chapters | Audience: Ages 7-10. | Audience: Grades 4 to 6.
Identifiers: LCCN 2017010739 (print) | LCCN 2017029184 (ebook) | ISBN 9781426329012 (e-book) | ISBN 9781426328992 (pbk. : alk. paper) | ISBN 9781426329005 (hardcover : alk. paper)
Subjects: LCSH: Animal behavior--Juvenile literature. | Pets--Juvenile literature.
Classification: LCC QL751.5 (ebook) | LCC QL751.5 .R36 2017 (print) | DDC 636.088/7--dc23
LC record available at https://lccn.loc.gov/2017010739

Printed in China
17/RRDS/1

Table of CONTENTS

Atticus destroys ... er ... *reads* the morning paper.

4

ATTICUS: ROWDY KITTY

Atticus paws at a box of cereal. Is he looking for a snack?

CRAZY KITTEN!

A red truck pulled up in front of the animal shelter in Fredericksburg, Virginia, U.S.A. Candice and Frank stepped out. They were both excited. For the first time in 25 years, they were getting a kitten. All of their older cats had died, and they felt their house had grown too quiet. They wanted a lively kitten. They headed inside the shelter to find one.

In one of the cat kennels, Candice spotted a black kitten with a fluffy tail. She picked him up. The kitten licked her chin. When Candice set him down, he attacked her shoe. So cute! This kitten certainly seemed lively. Candice and Frank agreed he would be their new pet. Before they even left the shelter, Candice named him Atticus (sounds like AT-ih-cuss). It seemed like a dignified name for a cat.

Candice and Frank filled out paperwork. They could pick up their new kitten the next day. They learned that Atticus and his sister had been found near a Dumpster. They were only four weeks old. Someone brought the kittens to the animal shelter. A foster family raised the kittens until they were old enough to be adopted.

The next day, Candice went back to the shelter. She tucked Atticus in his carrier and put it on the seat beside her. As she drove, she told Atticus he was going to a cozy house. "There are lace curtains on the windows," she said. "You'll have lots of places to sleep and interesting things to look at."

At home, Candice took the cat carrier inside. She unlatched the door. Atticus sprang out and started running on the wood floors. He ran and ran and ran. He ran upstairs and downstairs. He even clawed up Candice's back to the top of her head! "Ouch!" she said.

Atticus weighed only five pounds (2.3 kg). Yet when he ran, he sounded like a herd of wild horses. When he raced around a corner, his feet flew out from under him.

He skidded into the wall and kept going. Atticus ran so much, Candice wondered if he knew how to walk. He always seemed to be in a hurry. When she gave him some cat food, he gobbled it up. It was gone in two seconds flat.

That evening, Frank and Candice sat down to dinner. Atticus stared at them with round eyes. He smelled green beans and chicken cooked with mushrooms. Suddenly, he jumped straight up and grabbed a mushroom off Candice's plate. "That cat just ate a mushroom," Frank said in amazement.

That wasn't all Atticus ate. He nibbled on lettuce. He stuck his nose in Frank's coffee mug. He sipped tomato juice.

He licked the icing off cupcakes. Candice knew kittens needed a special diet, not people food. But Atticus was hard to stop. He jumped up on the kitchen counter to steal food. Candice and Frank had to store every morsel in chew-proof containers.

That didn't slow Atticus down. Soon he discovered the garbage can. Instead of tipping it over, he leaped right inside it. Once, Candice started to toss eggshells in the garbage can, and there was Atticus. He was sitting in potato peelings, looking up at her. To solve the problem, Candice bought a new garbage can with a foot-pedal lid.

During the first month, Atticus got into *everything*. Those pretty lace curtains on the windows? Atticus scaled them like ladders.

He shredded them to bits. He pulled the shades down to watch them snap back up again. So, Candice took the curtains and shades down from all the windows.

That didn't bother Atticus. He simply made up new games. He sat on tables and smacked books or drinking glasses onto the floor. Books made the best noises, but glasses made the biggest messes. Pens, rings, and keys were whacked under furniture. Candice and Frank had hoped a kitten would liven up their quiet house, but maybe Atticus was too lively.

Frank went off to work every day, but Candice worked at home. At least, she tried to. Keeping up with Atticus became her new full-time job. He still ran everywhere. He was on the go 24/7.

Black Cats

Black cats are
thought to be
lucky or unlucky,
depending on where—
and when—you live. In
ancient Egypt, people kept them
to gain favor with Bastet (sounds like
BAS-tet). She was the cat goddess.
But during the Middle Ages in Europe,
black cats were linked to witches.

You may have heard that it's unlucky
for a black cat to cross your path. In some
parts of England, it's lucky to own a black
cat but unlucky to meet one. Also, if a
black cat walks toward you, you'll have
good luck. But if it walks away from you,
it takes away your good luck!

Kittens are supposed to get tired easily and take lots of naps. Not Atticus. He never seemed to sleep. He had boundless energy.

Sometimes, Atticus disappeared. The first time he vanished, Candice worried he had slipped outside when she got the mail. "Atticus!" she called. No cat. She checked behind chairs and in corners. Then she peeked under the bed. Behind a box of shoes was a furry black shape. The cat was taking a hidden nap! So he *did* sleep, after all.

Stealing food, ripping curtains, and constantly running was typical kitten behavior. He would settle down as he got older, Candice knew. But Atticus had another issue. And this one was a real problem: He was a biter.

Like all kittens, Atticus loved to play. He played with toys. He played with Frank's and Candice's feet, too. Sometimes he scratched Candice on the ankle or bit Frank's hand. That was understandable. He would learn not to play so rough.

But Atticus bit when he wasn't playing. He seemed to attack them on purpose. His teeth broke their skin and left bruises. Each day, they added new bandages to their collection of bites.

Atticus's biting was a serious problem. Candice worried that a child might come visit. What if Atticus tried to attack? And that is just what happened.

ent

on In

ine.

70 KB

Atticus peeks out from behind a computer screen.

16

One December day, the doorbell rang. Atticus was sitting on a windowsill. He had never heard a doorbell before. He raced into Candice's home office. His eyes were wide with alarm. "It's just the doorbell," she told him. "It means we have company. Be on your best behavior, okay?" Atticus ran down the steps to the door so fast, his little legs were a blur.

Atticus's nose was pressed against the door as Candice tried to open it. Candice and Frank's neighbors stood on the porch. It was Michelle White and her three children: Gavin, Sydney, and Maren. Sydney held a fuzzy green mouse. "We're here to see the new kitty!" Michelle told Candice. "We brought him a present."

Since bringing Atticus home, Candice and Frank had only had a few guests. Candice wondered how Atticus would react to the children who were so excited to meet him. Gavin and Sydney got down on the floor to be closer to him. He sniffed their hands and feet. Then Gavin started to run down the hall. He wanted Atticus to play. This was a game Atticus knew! He raced after the boy. Meanwhile, Sydney ran in the other direction. Atticus was delighted to have two people to chase! He slid around the corner, his hind claws scrabbling before he hit the wall. Everyone laughed.

Gavin tossed the green mouse. Atticus pounced on it and kicked it with his back feet. "He's so cute!" said Sydney. Candice crossed her fingers. A fun game often turned rough with Atticus. She didn't quite trust him yet, especially around children.

Maren, who was only five, stood beside her mother. She squealed when Atticus leaped up in the air with the fuzzy mouse. Atticus stopped and stared at Maren. He trotted closer. Maren wanted to pet the soft kitten. But Candice knew that look in her kitty's eyes. When his pupils grew big, that meant watch out.

"Cat Goddess"

The ancient Egyptians believed cats were sacred (sounds like SAY-kred) animals. Only pharaohs (sounds like FAIR-ohs), or rulers, were allowed to own them. The Egyptians worshipped the cat goddess Bastet. Statues and paintings of her showed her as half woman, half cat.

Bastet's temple had a huge colony of cats. Cats that had died were brought there to be wrapped in linen sheets. They were buried as mummies. Sometimes mummy mice were buried with them.

Maren sensed danger, too. She ducked behind her mother's legs. Candice scooped up Atticus. "No!" she scolded him. "No biting!" She explained to her neighbor that Atticus had a problem with biting. "I don't want him to hurt anyone," she said.

Candice had prevented disaster. Afterward, she read books on cat behavior. She looked up information about cats on the Internet. How could she stop Atticus from biting? Putting him in the laundry room for a "time-out" didn't work. Atticus didn't remember what he had done wrong. Yelling at him didn't work.

Then Candice read that walking away from a misbehaving cat breaks the power the cat thinks he has. If there's no one to bite, the cat has to stop. The next time

Atticus acted up, she did just that. She walked away. An hour later, when she entered the kitchen, Atticus sprang at her. He bit her knee and dashed away.

"Our cat holds a *grudge*," Candice told Frank when he came home. "He remembered I walked away from him, and he bit me *later*. It's like he has to have the last word. Or, in his case, the last bite."

"Maybe this is a phase, and he'll outgrow it," Frank said.

But a few days later, Frank reached down to pet Atticus. The cat wrapped both paws around Frank's arm and bit his wrist, hard. Blood spurted from the wound. Frank's arm swelled, and his hand felt numb. Candice washed and wrapped Frank's wrist. This was serious.

She and her husband had worked with Atticus, but he was getting worse, not better. Atticus would have to go back to the animal shelter. He would have to be labeled a biter to warn families with children who might want to adopt him.

The next day, Candice put Atticus in the cat carrier. She drove to the animal shelter. But she didn't go in right away. In the parking lot, Candice cried. All her life, she had rescued cats from shelters and given them good homes. Now she was taking one *back*. In his carrier, Atticus looked around quietly. Most cats hate riding in cars. Often, they meow pitifully. But Atticus hadn't made a peep.

Candice got out and took Atticus inside the shelter. The director hurried over. Candice explained that she was bringing Atticus back because he wouldn't stop biting. The director looked at Atticus. "Hmm," she said. "Black cats aren't very popular, but he is very cute."

"Really? I love black cats." Candice said sadly. "I wish he didn't bite." The director told her the shelter didn't have room for Atticus right then. She suggested Candice bring him back in three days.

Back home, Atticus seemed to change. He became the sweetest cat. He didn't break anything. He didn't scratch or bite. He purred like a motorboat in Candice's lap. She couldn't believe he had changed.

When Frank came home from work that evening, he saw Atticus. "Weren't you taking him back today?" he asked. "He's been so good," Candice said. "Maybe driving him to the shelter scared him."

When the three days were up, she called the animal shelter. "We'll keep him after all," she said. Then Atticus winked one green eye and ran through the den, knocking over a potted plant. He whacked at a sofa cushion and gnawed the corner of the coffee table. Candice and Frank looked at each other. Their cat had not changed—not one single bit.

Atticus attacks a roll of toilet paper.

One morning, Candice was getting ready to go out. Atticus watched her take a tissue from the box. Hmmm. That looked interesting. He darted over to look at the box more closely. Then he began pulling tissues out with his teeth. One, two, three ... Candice quickly turned the box upside down before Atticus created a tissue blizzard.

Atticus also loved to attack rolls of toilet paper. Unlike most cats, Atticus loved water. His favorite room was the bathroom. He slept in the tub and napped in the sinks. He paddled his paws in the toilet to watch the water ripple. Once, when Frank was shaving, Atticus fell into the toilet. A very wet, very surprised cat streaked out of the bathroom.

His best trick was unrolling toilet paper. Atticus loved to sit on the toilet seat and smack the roll with his paws. *Smack, smack, smack* until the roll was empty. Then he'd grab one end of the toilet paper in his mouth and carry the long streamer all over the house.

Once Candice and Frank had decided to keep Atticus, they talked a lot about how to help him behave. All kittens are mischievous (sounds like MISS-chuh-vuss). Yet Atticus didn't seem to know any limits. "He has no manners," Candice said to Frank one evening at dinner. Atticus sat in the extra chair at the table. Candice and Frank were holding their plates high so he couldn't jump at them and steal food.

Candice knew cats could be trained. Atticus was smart. He *could* learn. He just didn't seem to want to. Candice took Atticus to the veterinarian (sounds like vet-er-ih-NAIR-ee-en). When Dr. Thompson picked up Atticus, he lay back in her arms, looking cute. She laughed. She examined him.

Did You Know?

Adult cats can sleep up to 16 hours a day. A three-year-old cat has been awake only one year of its life!

"He's part Persian. His coat will get much longer. And he has a lot of growing to do."

Candice hoped Atticus would grow *up,* too. She longed to put the curtains back on the windows and eat without holding her plate in the air. And *when* would he stop biting?

Back at home, Candice fed Atticus his lunch. She watched him as he ate. He was so small. He had lost his mother when he was very young. He didn't have an adult cat as a role model. Instead, Atticus must have thought *she* was his mother, his sister, and his playmate. And even his prey, when he wanted to hunt. He didn't understand that humans are not cats.

Then Candice read an article in a newspaper that said sometimes "only cats" are biters. She didn't want to get another cat. One was enough. But she learned from the article that playing with an only cat helped the cat release his energy. So, twice a day, Candice raced through the house dragging Atticus's long snake toy. She let him play as hard as he could. It was exhausting, but it seemed to help.

Months passed. Soon it was time for Candice to leave for her summer teaching job. When she returned six weeks later, she was in for a surprise. She no longer recognized Atticus. Whose cat was this? She had left behind a small, fluffy-tailed black kitten. Now he was a 13-pound (5.9-kg) longhaired cat. His coat wasn't all black anymore. Silver fur puffed around his neck, stomach, and hind legs.

"Does he still break things and bite?" she asked Frank. "A little," he replied.

The next day, Candice tried working in her office. Atticus chewed on her glasses. He stomped all over her computer keyboard. He erased the story she was writing!

Atticus was still Atticus. But he was also sweet. He lay in Candice's lap and purred. He no longer stole from the garbage can. He was still a biter, but mostly he bit shoes and door hinges.

Candice thought back to the day she'd picked out the little black kitten. "We almost sent you back to the shelter," she said to the cat who twirled around her legs. "I'm glad we didn't. You're part of the family." Atticus winked one green eye. No, he *ran* the family!

Cat Eyes

People used to think cats were color-blind. New research shows that cats are able to see blue, purple, yellow, and green. They don't see colors as brightly as humans do. But their world is not all shades of gray, either.

People also believed that cats could see in the dark. That's not entirely true. Cats can't see in total darkness, but they have better night vision than humans. The black part of the eye, called the pupil (sounds like PYOO-puhl), grows very wide in dim light. This lets a cat's eye take in more light and see more.

Peepers and a friend nibble on treats left for them on the ground.

PEEPERS:
EMU
THIEF

A visitor feeds Peepers a handful of broccoli.

TROUBLE WITH A "P"

A car rumbled down a bumpy road in Orange County, Virginia, U.S.A. The back seat held a cage with two strange birds inside. The birds gawked out the window while the car made its way to a gated area. At the gates, a woman was waiting to meet them. The driver handed the cage over to her, then drove off. "Welcome to Rikki's," she said to the birds.

The woman gently placed the cage on the seat of her truck and began driving the rest of the way up the road. Green leafy bushes brushed the sides of the truck. The truck stopped in front of a white building. The woman picked up the cage and carried it inside.

She set the cage on the floor and unlatched the door. The birds stepped out onto the bare floor. They both had long necks and long legs and brown-and-cream-striped feathers.

A tabby cat stared down at the newcomers from a carpeted perch against the wall. Another cat lay draped across a desk. The cats narrowed their eyes.

The woman was a volunteer (sounds like vol-uhn-TEER) at Rikki's. She filled a heavy dog dish with water and scattered straw on the floor. "This is your new home," she said with a smile. "Enjoy!" Then she left to tend to her other chores.

Rikki's Refuge (sounds like REF-yooj) is a sanctuary for animals that are old, or sick, or otherwise unadoptable (sounds like un-uh-DOP-tuh-buhl). Rikki's opened in 1996 for rescue cats and dogs. The large property is now home to cows, pigs, rabbits, chickens, geese, sheep, turkeys, goats, peacocks, and about 600 cats. Oh! And now two emus (sounds like EE-myoos) named Peepers and Phoebe (sounds like FEE-bee).

Peepers and his sister Phoebe began life as a school project in Manassas (sounds like muh-NASS-us), Virginia. Their eggs were hatched in an incubator (sounds like IN-kyuh-bey-ter). Excited students watched the eggs crack open. The birds inside looked a little like ostriches (sounds like AH-strih-jez). Two weeks later, one lucky student took the baby emus home, hoping to keep them. But the emus were already eight inches (20.3 cm) tall and would get much, much taller. They would soon become too hard to care for. So the family brought them to Rikki's Refuge instead.

Now Peepers and Phoebe looked around their new home. They poked their beaks into a cat food dish. The cats glared at them. *Not yours*, they seemed to say. The door opened and another volunteer came in, lugging sacks of cat litter. Peepers raced over on his long legs. He followed the volunteer around like a puppy.

This building was the refuge's main office. Donations (sounds like doh-NEY-shuns) of food and supplies were brought here. The office was a busy place. Volunteers came and went with their list of chores for the day. Feeding and caring for more than a thousand animals was a lot of work.

It would take some time for the young emus to adjust to their new home. They snapped their beaks at the cats that hissed at them. They fell into their water dish. They got into things. The emus were more curious than cats! And more trouble.

A Different Bird

Emus are part of a group of birds called ratites (sounds like RAT-ights). They are flightless birds. Other birds in this group are the ostrich, kiwi, rhea (sounds like REE-uh), and cassowary (sounds like KAS-uh-wer-ee), which is shown above. The emu is the second largest bird in the world, after the ostrich. Emus are native to Australia, where they live in the desert and grasslands. Emus eat grass, fruit, seeds, and insects.

Adult emus can grow to be six feet (1.8 m) tall and weigh up to 130 pounds (59 kg). Females are slightly bigger than males. Long-legged emus can run more than 30 miles an hour (48.3 km/h) and travel great distances.

The director of Rikki's, Kerry Hilliard (sounds like HILL-yard), decided the birds needed to be outdoors. A large pen was built just for them. The emus had plenty of space to run around, dirt to take dust baths in, and a plastic pool to wade in. Within months, Peepers and Phoebe had almost reached their full height of six feet (1.8 m). Long, soft plumes had replaced their brown and cream feathers. They were beautiful. And soon, they became the stars of the refuge. Everyone wanted to visit the friendly, curious birds.

One day, Kerry went into Emu Estates, as they had named the pen. Peepers ran right up to her and snatched off her glasses. "Hey!" she yelled. Then Peepers ran into an area thick with grass and trees.

"Peepers!" she called. "Get back here!"

Peepers came running back, but without Kerry's glasses in his beak. "Where are my glasses?" she asked him. Kerry couldn't see without her glasses! How would she find them? She looked around the tall grass with no luck. She felt too embarrassed to ask anyone for help. What would she say? A great big bird stole her glasses and wouldn't give them back?

But Peepers kept nudging her with his head. Kerry realized that he was trying to *show* her where he'd put her glasses! It was a game! Who would believe this huge bird wanted to play?

That wasn't the only game Peepers wanted to play. The wire fence in Emu Estates needed repairing. A volunteer went

there with his tools.
He lay wire cutters,
pliers (sounds like
PLY-ers), screwdrivers,
and a hammer on the
ground. The shiny metal tools
glinted in the sun. Peepers couldn't
resist. When the man's back was turned,
Peepers grabbed the pliers and hid them in
the bushes.

Then he took the wire cutters and hid
them in the tall grass. Next he took a
screwdriver. The man turned around for
his tools, but they were gone! Peepers crept
up behind him. Then the man caught
Peepers in the act of stealing another
screwdriver. The word was out. Peepers
was a thief. What would he steal next?

Peepers steals a shiny ribbon
from a visitor's pocket!

PICKPOCKET PEEPERS

A group of people waited at the gate of Rikki's Refuge. The June breeze stirred some wildflowers growing beside the road. Today was tour day at the refuge. The refuge is normally not open to the public, but three or four days a month, people are allowed to tour it. Today's tour would be extra exciting. This tour would include the emus.

The visitors carried donations of dog food, cat food, cat litter, paper towels, trash bags, and other much needed supplies. Some had also brought treats—crackers for the cows and cookies for the goats and sheep. Sometimes a visitor would bring broccoli for the emus, but not today.

Lolly Busey (sounds like BYOO-see), the volunteer in charge of tours, greeted them. "Please stay together," she said, leading the group onto the grounds. Cats napped under trees. Roosters and chickens strutted back and forth. Geese waddled around them, honking. Goats trotted over, hoping for cookies. Peacocks spread their magnificent tails.

Did You Know?

When emus run, they hold their small wings out for balance.

"Who wants to see the emus first?" asked Lolly. Everyone did.

She unlatched the first door to Emu Estates. People squeezed in, and Lolly latched the door behind them. Then she unlatched the second door. This two-door system prevented the birds from escaping. Emu are very fast runners!

A woman and her teenage daughter were the first inside Emu Estates. Peepers scooted right over and stood very close to the woman. He was taller than she was. He stared at her with his brown eyes. Nervous, the woman backed up. "Peepers won't hurt you," Lolly reassured her. "He's quite friendly."

Peepers waited for the woman to offer him a bunch of broccoli. It was his favorite treat. He didn't see any. But he did see a

shiny gold watch around her wrist.
He bent his long neck and, with a snip of
his beak, slipped the watch right off her
wrist! "Oh!" the woman exclaimed. Then
Peepers took off, his long legs eating up
the ground as he ran into the bushes.

Lolly hurried after him. "Peepers!"
she yelled. "Bring that back right now!"
At the sound of her voice, the emu
stopped. Lolly took the watch from
him and returned it to the woman.
What on earth is wrong with that bird?
she wondered. Then she told everyone
the story about how the emus had come
to live at Rikki's. As everyone listened,
Peepers's sister Phoebe came closer.
The woman and her daughter admired
the bird's beautiful feathers.

Birds of a Feather

Emus can't fly. They are too heavy, and their wings are too small. Instead of flying away from enemies, these birds use their powerful legs to run very fast.

Birds that fly have hollow bones, which makes them light in the air. An emu's bones are solid. Flying birds need strong, stiff feathers to push against the air. Emu feathers are soft and fluffy. They are called plumes. For many years, people hunted birds like emus for their plumes. People used the plumes for hats, coats, and costumes.

Peepers moved over toward the teenage daughter. A glittery barrette held back the girl's brown hair. The hair clip sparkled in the sun. Peepers blinked his long eyelashes. Then, before anyone could stop him, he yanked the barrette out of the girl's hair and ran. The girl shrieked. Once again, Lolly chased after the emu and collected the barrette. "I don't know what's the matter with him today," she said, apologizing to the visitors.

On the next tour day, an older woman stepped into Emu Estates, eager to see the exotic birds. Peepers stalked right up to her. He took one look at her shiny gold necklace and grabbed it. The necklace wouldn't come loose. Peepers ran anyway, pulling the woman with him! "Eek!"

the woman screeched. "Peepers, stop!" Lolly ordered. He did, but reluctantly.

A young girl wearing big gold hoop earrings arrived at the end of the tour. Peepers stomped over to her. He tipped his head, looking at her. The swaying, shiny circles fascinated him. Then he snapped his beak forward to nab an earring. The girl clapped one hand over her ear. She held on to the earring as he tugged, so he wouldn't hurt her. This time Lolly had brought some broccoli. She thrust the bunch at him, and he let go of the girl's earring. He chewed thoughtfully on the broccoli, but he was still staring at the earring.

After the group left, Lolly went back into Emu Estates. She tossed Peepers a few vanilla wafers. "What is the matter with you?" she asked. Peepers didn't answer, of course. He stared into her eyes and blinked. Then he wrapped his long neck around hers, giving Lolly an emu hug. Lolly smiled. It was hard not to love Peepers. But it was also clear that Peepers was a problem.

From then on, Lolly Busey warned tour groups. "Don't wear bracelets, necklaces, dangly earrings, or shiny barrettes. Our emu Peepers loves anything sparkly, and he will steal them! And watch out for your glasses, too!"

The tours went smoothly after that. But Peepers missed his glittery treasures.

One afternoon a group entered Emu Estates. Lolly wasn't available that day, so a young man led the tour. Peepers eyed

the visitors carefully. No watches.
No necklaces. No barrettes. He studied
an older man. Then the man bent down to
tie his shoelace. Peepers noticed something
glittering in the man's back pocket.

Quick as lightning, Peepers picked the
man's pocket. He fished out a gold money
clip with dollar bills. Then he ran across
the field with his prize. The volunteer, who
was wise to Peepers's tricks, was a pretty
fast runner himself. He caught up to the
bird and snatched the money clip back.
He returned it to the astonished visitor.

What to do about Peepers? All the
visitors wanted to see the emus. Phoebe
was good, but Peepers simply couldn't
be trusted. He wasn't just a thief. He was
also a pickpocket!

Peepers and a pig friend wait for the new mudhole to be dug at the refuge.

Chapter 3

EVERYBODY IN THE POOL

Before long, the big birds got some company. Several potbellied pigs moved into Emu Estates. People buy these pigs because they are little and cute. But pigs don't always stay that way. Some grow too big for their owners to handle. That's how Teddy, Millie, Jeb, Roxie, Sherman, and other potbellies found themselves at their new home at Rikki's Refuge.

Peepers, Phoebe, and the pigs got along just fine. Everyone at Rikki's hoped Peepers wouldn't be tempted to steal food with the other animals around. Each day, the volunteers filled the pigs' trough (sounds like TRAWF). Eager to eat, the pigs walked under their buckets. Some of the grain spilled out and fell onto their backs. Peepers pecked the grain right off their backs, as if the pigs were dinner tables.

Next, a 700-pound (318-kg) hog named Petunia joined the group. The director, Kerry Hilliard, realized the plastic wading pool wasn't big enough for all the animals. Hogs and pigs *and* emus love water. They needed a bigger, deeper mudhole.

One weekend, a group of volunteers arrived to help dig a new hole. A

husband-and-wife
team emptied the
wading pool with
buckets so it could
be moved. When the
man stooped over to
scoop out the last of the
water, someone leaned over
his shoulder. Hot breath blew in his
ear. Then he felt his earlobe being
nibbled. The man straightened up and
came face-to-face with a huge bird.
Peepers grunted as the man stepped back
in surprise.

Another volunteer started to dig the
pit with a backhoe. Peepers and Phoebe
scooted away. The potbellied pigs didn't
like the racket, either. When the pit was

finished, the man unrolled a hose and began filling the mudhole with water. The emus and pigs charged out of their hiding places, excited by the sight of so much water!

Before the pool was filled, the pigs decided to take a swim. Peepers and Phoebe had the same idea. They nearly ran over the pigs to be the first ones in! *Splish! Splash!* The emus bobbed and floated, their feathers fluffed up around them. The pigs slid in next. The man filled the pool to the top.

Peepers eyed the shiny brass nozzle (sounds like NOZ-uhl) on the end of the hose. He hadn't stolen anything in a long time. Now was his chance. He paddled over to the man and nabbed the hose right out of his hand! The hose sprayed water into the air, giving Peepers and the others a shower. What a fun day!

Word got out that Rikki's Refuge took in emus. People in the area who had tried raising emus, and found that it wasn't that easy, dropped off their birds. They knew the birds would be safe at Rikki's. Other emus were picked up wandering down nearby roads or running loose in fields, fully grown and homeless. Soon 10 emus, including Phoebe and Peepers, called Emu Estates their home.

Did You Know?

Emus are excellent swimmers and love to play in water.

Strange Stomachs

All birds have two-part stomachs. The main part is like a human's stomach. The second part is a pouch, called a gizzard. Gizzards help birds digest their food.

Some birds, like emus, ducks, doves, turkeys, and quail, have gizzards with thick walls. These birds swallow gravel and small pebbles. The rocks and gravel collect in the gizzard. The strong muscles of the gizzard, along with the stones, grind up food so it can be digested.

Emus have been known to swallow marbles, bottle caps, watches, and even wire. They hide these objects to swallow later. It is important to keep their enclosure free of loose metal objects that may become stuck in their gizzards.

Peepers and Phoebe welcomed the other emus. Peepers especially perked up. At last, he could run real races against other emus. Humans were just too slow. He taught the other emus how to race the volunteers. He showed the birds how to run ahead just a little, to fool people into thinking they might win the race. Then he'd speed up. When Peepers reached the finish line that only he knew about, he'd give the person a glance as if to say, *Slowpoke!* All the emus became good at this game.

Peepers also taught the others how to play "shadow." First, he would sneak up behind someone. When the person turned around, Peepers would move his head from side to side, always staying

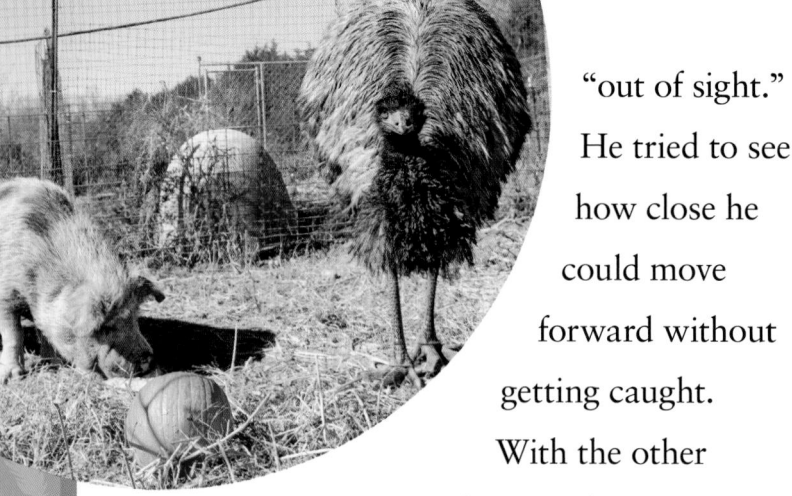

"out of sight."
He tried to see
how close he
could move
forward without
getting caught.
With the other
animals around, Lolly noticed
that Peepers wasn't being as naughty. But
he still loved tour day. And he was still the
star of Rikki's Refuge.

One evening, Lolly visited Emu Estates
alone. She stood outside the fence and
looked in. The potbellied pigs lay chest-
deep in mud at the edge of the pool.
Petunia the hog snored under a tree.
Peepers and an emu named Steve were
racing along the far side of the pen.

The other male emu, Marty, joined Peepers and Steve in a game of three-way tag. Above, a full moon rose over the treetops.

The female emus had ducked into the brush. Then Lolly heard something. *Thrummm! Thrumm! THRUMMM!*

The female emus made a loud booming sound deep in their throats like a drum. Most of the male emus stopped running and stared into the bushes. The females had gotten their attention!

Peepers didn't notice. He folded his long legs and settled on the ground. Another tour day would come soon. Maybe an unsuspecting guest would come in wearing something sparkly.

Meet Coco! She looks sweet ... but don't be fooled.

COCO:
TERRIER
TROUBLE

Coco enjoys rolling in the grass.

Chapter 1

PERFECT DOG?

The couple stood in front of a pet store in Kansas City, Kansas, U.S.A. Michelle Meade-Esvang bit her lip. She and her husband, Richard, loved dogs. She wanted a puppy. She was looking for a breed of dog called West Highland white terrier (sounds like TARE-ee-er). They had looked for a long time. Would she find the dog of her dreams here?

Michelle had already looked at the animal shelter for a dog like this. They were nicknamed Westies (sounds like WES-tees). She saw a dog there that she liked, but that dog didn't even look at her. That dog was not for them.

Now she paused at the door of the pet store. Getting a new dog sounded easy enough, but finding the *right* dog was not.

"Remember Cosmo?" Michelle asked Richard. "He was the perfect dog."

Cosmo was a Westie they had had a long time ago. He was a good dog. He learned quickly. He didn't bark nearly as much as most terriers do. He was also very cute. When they

Did You Know?

Centuries ago, people believed that white dogs weren't as smart as dogs of different colors.

took Cosmo out for walks, people stopped on the sidewalk and asked to pet him.

Michelle bought Cosmo a stuffed toy that looked like a little Westie. When Cosmo snuggled next to his stuffed Westie, she could barely tell them apart. Yes, Cosmo was perfect.

Then her husband said, "Remember Skippy?" *Oh, yes,* Michelle thought. *Skippy.* He was not perfect. In fact, Skippy was the opposite of perfect.

After Cosmo died, Michelle really wanted another dog just like him. She decided to rescue another Westie from a terrier adoption agency. Before long, she got a phone call from the agency. They had a Westie that needed a home. Did Michelle want the dog? "Yes," Michelle said. "I do!"

There was one problem, the lady from the agency told her. The dog had already had three owners. That was a lot of owners. *How bad could one small dog be?* Michelle wondered.

She contacted the man who was giving the "problem" Westie away. The dog's name was Skippy. He lived far away from Michelle. Michelle and the man agreed to meet halfway so he could give her Skippy.

They decided to meet in the parking lot of the Topeka Zoo. Michelle thought that was an odd place to meet, but figured the parking lot was far away from the animals. It should be okay.

The zoo parking lot was crowded, but she found the man with Skippy. Skippy was a wiggly bundle of white fur. The man tried to hand Skippy to her. Before Michelle had a tight grip, the dog squirted out of her arms like soap. Then he raced straight for the zoo entrance! Westies have short legs, but they are made to *run*. Down the asphalt path the little dog streaked, darting between people and strollers. Michelle ran after him, but the dog was faster.

"Help me! My dog is loose!" she cried to a zoo employee. "Dogs aren't allowed in the zoo!" he yelled.

Michelle caught sight of a white blur just past the giraffe enclosure (sounds like en-KLOH-zhur). "Skippy!" she called. "Come back!" Skippy either didn't know his name, or he didn't want to stop. Michelle ran faster, her heart pounding. Skippy was headed right for the lions!

A Special Breed

West Highland white terriers are a special breed, or kind, of dog. The word "terrier" comes from the Latin word *terra,* which means "earth." So terriers are "earth dogs." They are small, short-legged, and white. Westies don't seem to know they are small. They stand up to the biggest dogs without fear.

Westies originally came from Scotland. Long ago, farmers used the small, brave dogs to hunt and kill rats that ate their grain. With their stubby little legs, Westies could climb hills to find rats hiding among the rocks. Today, Westies are usually pets, not working dogs.

Suddenly, a man stepped in and scooped up the runaway Westie. Michelle's knees were weak when she finally caught up. Gratefully, she took Skippy from his rescuer and hurried back through the zoo to her car. "You could have been a lion's dinner!" she said to the dog.

She drove home. The moment she let Skippy indoors, he tore from room to room like a jungle beast. Michelle's son, Arden, immediately jumped up on the sofa. He wanted to get away from the crazy terrier.

When the dog went to the bathroom on the floor, Michelle realized Skippy was not housebroken. Richard let Skippy out into their fenced-in backyard. Maybe he'd go to the bathroom outside.

Instead, Skippy disappeared. The house had a tall privacy fence, with the boards nailed close together. Skippy couldn't have slipped between those boards.

He hadn't dug under the fence, either. Michelle and Richard walked every inch of the fence and didn't find any holes. Skippy was just ... gone.

Half an hour later, Skippy trotted up to the back door and scratched on it to be let in. "Where have you been?" Michelle said. For an answer, Skippy peed on the carpet.

Unfortunately, this became Skippy's pattern. He ran around the house wildly. He never came when his name was called. He vanished from the backyard. And he could not be trained to go to the bathroom outside. Not good.

Michelle worked with Skippy, but
she worried he would never settle down.
Maybe their house wasn't big enough for
such a lively, stubborn dog. She gave
Skippy to a girl who lived on a farm. There,
he would have plenty of room to run.

But the Esvang family still wanted a
dog. Michelle had her heart set on a
Westie. Taking a deep breath, she pushed
open the door to the pet store. Richard
followed. They looked around.

There, sitting in a cage, was a West
Highland white terrier puppy. The puppy
thumped its tail, and Michelle put
her hand to her chest. He was adorable.
Could this Westie be the perfect dog?

With her leash on,
Coco is ready to go.

Chapter 2

SNEAKY COCO

The little female dog was the size of a toaster. Her furry white coat stuck out all over like dandelion (sounds like DAN-dee-LIE-uhn) fluff. Michelle took the dog out of the cage. The Westie licked her face, giving her sweet puppy kisses. Michelle giggled. "Guess what?" she said to her husband. "We have a new dog! Her name is ... Coco!"

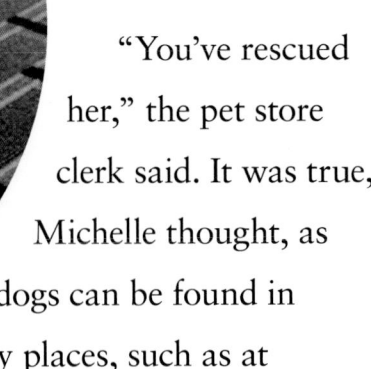

"You've rescued her," the pet store clerk said. It was true, Michelle thought, as dogs can be found in many places, such as at animal shelters, through pet adoption organizations, and in pet stores. They bought Coco a new collar, food and water dishes, a leash, a bed, and toys.

In the car, Coco sat in Michelle's lap. Most dogs would stare out the window at the passing scenery or wiggle around. But Coco licked Michelle's hands and face all the way home. *Such a good dog,* Michelle thought. *A good, sweet dog.* She had made the right choice.

Arden got his first glimpse of the new

dog when he got home from school that day. Coco sat on a towel on the sofa. She didn't jump down and run wildly like Skippy had done. She didn't bark. She just sat there, looking adorable.

Her little white tail stuck up like a carrot. Her ears were furry white triangles. Her black nose was like a gumdrop.

Coco's dark brown eyes took in everything. At the sight of Arden, her pink tongue fell out of her mouth in a doggy grin. Then she crouched in a playing position and rolled off the couch. Michelle laughed. Was there anything funnier than a new puppy?

But Michelle worried when the sun went down and it grew dark outside. This would be Coco's first night in her new home. Often puppies cry at night when they are in a new place because they are lonely. So Michelle placed a large cage with Coco's soft bed and water dish inside next to her side of the bed. Coco trotted inside, curled up in her bed, and went to sleep. No crying, no barking. No scratching to get out. *Now that's a good dog!* Michelle thought.

The next day, Coco looked around the apartment. She nosed in corners and sniffed at the furniture. Michelle took her out on her leash. Outside, Coco came to life! She had not been trained to walk on a leash. So she sprinted down the sidewalk. Michelle was barely able to keep up.

The pet store offered a training class. Michelle took Coco to "school."

Dogs of all shapes and sizes came to the training ring in the center of the store. The first lesson was to learn to walk on a leash beside the owner and not run ahead. At first, Coco ran around in circles, winding the leash around Michelle's legs. Michelle turned around and around to unwind herself.

The dog owners held a treat in one fist. Each time their dog obeyed a command, the animal was given a treat as a reward. Coco loved her treats! She learned to walk on the leash *and* sit, all in one day! Michelle couldn't believe it.

Did You Know?

The name West Highland white terrier was officially given in 1909, in America. Before then, the breed had several other names, such as Roseneath, Poltalloch, and Pittenweem.

Beyond "Bowwow"

Dogs talk to us, and we talk to them. But can dogs understand us? Or do they just hear "Blah, blah, blah"? Over the years, dogs and humans have often worked together. Dogs herd sheep, and other animals. They pull sleds and hunt birds. Dogs can be trained to respond to commands, like "sit" and "stay." Some dogs can understand more than simple commands. Chase, a border collie, knew the names of over a thousand objects!

How do dogs learn words? Trainers may need to repeat the word for an object 20 to 40 times before a dog learns it!

At home, though, Coco forgot her lessons. She still walked too far ahead on the leash. She sat when she was told, but only sometimes. And only if she got *several* treats. One day, Coco decided she would walk herself! She picked up the leash in her mouth and jogged along beside Michelle.

Soon it was time for Coco's first bath. When Michelle picked her up from the groomer, Coco wore bows between her ears. She did *not* like being dressed up. The bows didn't last long. She shook her head until they flew off. The puppy was becoming more independent (sounds like in-dih-PEN-dunt).

One day Arden came home from school and wanted to play his video game. The cord that attached to the computer was missing. Then he realized that the power cord wasn't just missing. It had been sliced off the game console. How did that happen?

He looked across the room. Coco sat on her towel on the sofa, gnawing one of her chew toys. "Did you do this?" he asked. Coco looked up at him with her dark brown eyes. *Not me,* she seemed to say. *I'm perfect!* Arden wasn't so sure. To be safe, he wrapped duct tape around all the cords on his electronic devices.

More strange things began to happen around the apartment, Michelle noticed. She found one of Richard's shoes dragged out of the closet. It had been chewed on. The tug-of-war stuffed monkey had lost its arms and legs. The brand-new hedgehog stuffie didn't even last a day.

Was Coco forgetting her training? Michelle wondered. Had she ever learned those lessons to begin with?

Michelle had good reason to wonder. She was leaving for Virginia, U.S.A., for six weeks to go to school. She was going to finish getting a degree. Richard taught classes in the summer, and Arden was attending camp. Six weeks was too long to board a dog. Michelle would have to take Coco with her.

That should be all right. After all, her dog seemed very well-behaved. What could possibly happen?

Coco visits the motel near Hollins University for the first time.

COCO GOES TO COLLEGE

Michelle drove from the flat lands of Kansas to the mountains of Virginia. Coco enjoyed the trip.

She sniffed the air, enjoying the new smells of forests and deer.

Dogs couldn't stay in the apartments on the campus of Hollins (sounds like HOL-inz) University. So, Michelle found a nearby motel that allowed dogs.

Their room was on the ground floor, toward the back of the motel. It had two double beds, a dresser with a TV, a closet, and a bathroom. It would be Michelle and Coco's home for the next six weeks.

Coco was eight months old now and needed lots of exercise. Michelle would be in class all day. What would Coco do?

Early the next morning, Michelle walked Coco on the grassy hill behind the motel. Back in their room, Michelle played tug with Coco. Then she had to get ready for class.

When Michelle returned to the motel, it was evening. Coco bounded over to greet her. Michelle noticed white flakes on the carpet by the door. Strange. She took Coco outside for a walk but was too tired to play with her.

The next morning, Michelle discovered bits of leather all over the floor. Her best sandals had been destroyed. "You're supposed to be a good dog," Michelle said.

After class that evening, she found more mysterious white flakes on the floor. She looked at the white door. Were those scratch marks near the bottom?

The mystery of the white flakes was solved the next day. As Michelle got ready to leave, Coco scrabbled at the door. Her claws scraped off a blizzard of white paint. "No, Coco!" Michelle scolded. How could she keep the dog from ruining the door?

The next time Michelle came into the motel room, she spotted a hole in the blue carpet by the door. The motel was fairly old. Maybe the hole had always been there. But each day, the hole grew bigger.

One afternoon, Michelle saw a long blue thread trailing across the floor. At the other end of the thread was Coco. Michelle trimmed the thread, hoping Coco would leave the rug alone. Nope. Coco found that the mesh-like material under the carpet was even more fun. She grabbed it with her teeth and pulled it up in pieces. Soon, the bare cement floor was exposed! If Coco kept wrecking the motel room, Michelle would have to pay a lot for damages.

It was obvious that Coco couldn't stay locked in the room all day. At school, Michelle found two teenage girls who offered to walk Coco around campus for a few hours.

Coco loved going to college! She flew across the thick, green lawn. She plowed through the grass with her nose. Then her ears perked. Ants! She snuffled and snorted until the ants were snagged in the fur around her face. Her tongue darted out as she ate every one. "Ewww," said her dog walkers.

But the girls couldn't walk Coco every day. Michelle knew Coco was unhappy. She played with Coco and threw tennis balls as often as she could. But it didn't seem to matter. Coco was still unhappy. She ruined another pair of Michelle's sandals.

Michelle also found more white crumbs by the door. She glanced down at the door frame. The frame was made of a substance called stucco (sounds like STUHK-oh).

Bringing Home a Puppy

Getting ready for a new puppy? Here are some tips to prepare your home for the new member of your family.

Puppies are naturally curious and get into everything. They like to explore with their mouths and will chew anything. Make sure there are no dangerous items the puppy can reach, like cords, plugs, plants, cleaning supplies, even holiday decorations. Small toys can choke a small dog. Put these things away.

Use childproof locks on lower cabinet doors. Keep basement doors and

second-story windows closed. Store trash in a can with a lid.

If you live in a house with a yard, there should be a sturdy fence. Terriers and many other types of dogs love to dig under fences or squeeze between the boards. Keep them safe!

Coco had chewed a huge chunk right out of the wall! Michelle's perfect dog was trashing the motel room!

Coco's bad behavior grew worse. One evening, Michelle unlocked the motel door, juggling a basket of clean clothes. Coco shot outside. She raced through the parking lot and around to the front of the motel. Michelle could not catch her. What if Coco ran out onto the highway? Then she heard shouting. Some women who worked in the motel's laundry waved their arms as a small white dog raced back and forth. Michelle hurried over and captured Coco.

After that, Coco tried to make a break for it whenever Michelle opened the door. And each day, Michelle found more wall-chewing, carpet-pulling, and door-scraping. She cleaned up the white paint flakes on the floor. She duct-taped the hole in the carpet. At the rate Coco was going, there wouldn't *be* a motel room at the end of six weeks.

Arden got out of camp and flew to Virginia to join his mother. Coco was thrilled to see him. She jumped and wagged her carrot tail. "I have so much homework," Michelle said to her son. "*Please* keep Coco busy." Arden played with Coco for what seemed like a thousand hours. Then he went with his mother to the campus.

That evening when they returned, their room was a mess. Arden's best earbuds were in shreds. Covers had been yanked off the beds. Holes were chewed in a book bag. In the middle of it all, Coco happily pushed around two tennis balls. Michelle's heart sank. What had happened to her good dog?

But suddenly she realized that to Coco, the motel room was like the cage in the pet store. She scratched at the door and the carpet and even the wall because she wanted *out*. Coco missed her family. She wanted to be with them.

Michelle picked up Coco, who gave her sweet dog kisses. School would be over soon, and they would all go home. Coco didn't have to be perfect. She only had to be her sweet, funny self. And that was good enough.

THE END

DON'T MISS!

NATIONAL GEOGRAPHIC KiDS **CHAPTERS**

DOG ON A BIKE!

And More True Stories of Amazing Animal Talents!

Moira Rose Donohue

Turn the page for a sneak preview . . .

Is that a dog on a bike? Yes! It's Norman.

NORMAN: DOG ON A BIKE!

Norman takes a spin around the block.

Chapter 1

A DOG STAR IS BORN

Something is moving at the end of the block. And it's coming closer. Is it a bear on skates? A Wookie on wheels? No, it's Norman, a Briard (sounds like bree-ARD). And he's riding a bike!

What's a Briard? It's a very shaggy dog. The breed came from France. But Norman isn't just any Briard. He's a superstar dog.

Norman can ride a bike all by himself. He hangs his fuzzy front paws over the handlebars. Then he pushes the pedals with his back feet. And off he goes, fur flying! True, the bike still has training wheels. But he's not even six years old yet!

It all started years ago. Norman is owned by Karen Cobb. She's a professional (sounds like pro-FESH-eh-nahl) dog trainer. Her father was a vet, so she grew up around animals. But she never had her own pet dog. After she finished college, Karen got a dog of her own. It was a Shiba Inu (sounds like SHEE-buh EE-noo). She wanted him to be very well trained. So she read every dog training book she could find. She took classes, and she began teaching him.

She didn't know it, but Shiba Inus pick and choose which commands they obey. That makes them hard to train. Teaching him basic obedience (sounds like oh-BEE-DEE-ens) skills, like "come" and "watch," was a challenge. It was also difficult to teach him agility skills, like running through a tunnel and weaving between poles. But she kept working at it. Eventually, he came in first place for his breed in the entire country!

Karen was hooked on dog training. She wanted to do it for her job. So she took more classes and worked at a dog training company. That's when she first met a Briard named Norman. Norman's owners wanted Karen to train him.

Briards are big, lovable oafs. They weigh about 75 pounds (34 kg). They have long, wavy fur. Some have ears that stand up. They love to jump and bounce. Briards are herding dogs. They stay very close to their owners. That makes them easy to train. And although they often act like clowns, these goofballs are supersmart and very loyal. Karen wanted to own one. But by then, she had two Shiba Inus. She would have to wait to get another dog.

Karen opened her own dog training school. She had a busy life with her family, her business, and her dogs. Finally, after many years, she knew it was the right time to get a Briard. She researched all the breeders and found the one she liked best. This breeder was in Washington State,

U.S.A. Karen called her.

"I want a dog that is gentle but one that really wants to learn," she told the breeder. The breeder understood. But she said it might be a while. That was OK. Karen was willing to wait until just the right litter came along. After all, it's not every day that a star is born.

In fact, it took another year and a half before the breeder thought she had the right litter of pups. Karen flew out to meet the puppies. There were four that were "show quality." That means they could compete in dog shows. The breeder put different-colored collars on those four so that Karen could identify them.

"Here, fetch!" Karen said as she threw toys to the four pups. She watched to see who wanted to play.

Then she ran and hid. She waited to see who would come to find her. Two pups did. They seemed to be the most curious. But the one with the blue collar was gentler.

"Come here, boy," she said. He bounded up to her. She ruffled his fluffy fur. Karen knew then that he was the one. It had been a long wait, but worth it. Can you guess what she named him? Norman, after the first Briard in her life!

Norman was about to begin his new life with Karen. But first, he had to travel to Georgia, U.S.A., where Karen lived. It was almost 2,000 miles (3,219 km) away. He would have to fly on a plane.

Someone to Watch Over Me

Herding dogs are bred to work on farms and ranches. They move livestock from one place to another. They can make sheep and cattle head in the right direction. They bark and chase them around. And when that doesn't work, they nip them. German shepherds are herding dogs. So are border collies and, of course, Briards. Corgis (sounds like KOR-geese) herd, too, even though they are only about one foot (30.5 cm) tall at the shoulder . . .

Want to know what happens next? Be sure to check out *Dog on a Bike!* Available wherever books and ebooks are sold.

INDEX

Boldface indicates illustrations.

MORE INFORMATION

To find more information about the animal species featured in this book, check out these books, magazine articles, websites, and videos.

How to Speak Cat: A Guide to Decoding Cat Language, by Aline Alexander Newman and Gary Weitzman, National Geographic, 2015.

Emu, by Claire Saxby, Candlewick, 2015.

West Highland White Terriers, by Dominique De Vito, Animal Planet Pet Care Library, 2009.

National Geographic, "Animals: Domestic Cat" **nationalgeographic.com/ animals/mammals/d/ domestic-cat**

National Geographic, "Cats Rule in Ancient Egypt" **kids.nationalgeographic .com/explorecats-rule-in -ancient-egypt**

San Diego Zoo Animals & Plants, "Emu" **animals.sandiegozoo.org/ animals/emu**

Rikki's Refuge Animal Sanctuary **rikkisrefuge.org**

Westie Rescue USA **westierescue.com**

CREDITS

This book is for Kerry Hilliard, the staff, and the volunteers who dedicate their time at Rikki's Refuge Animal Sanctuary. —CR

ACKNOWLEDGMENTS

Heartfelt thanks to:

My husband, Frank, a dog person who became a cat person.

Michelle Meade-Esvang and her son, Arden, who let me interview them and take photos of the charming Coco.

Lolly Busey, director of administration volunteer/tour coordinator at Rikki's Refuge Animal Sanctuary, who gave me an eye-opening tour of Rikki's Refuge, let me take photos, and provided more photographs of Peepers.

A special thanks to Brenna Maloney, freelance project editor at National Geographic Kids Books, who guided me with kindness and expertise through the editorial process.

Thanks also to Shelby, Kathryn, Sarah, and Sanjida for helping produce a book I'm truly proud of!